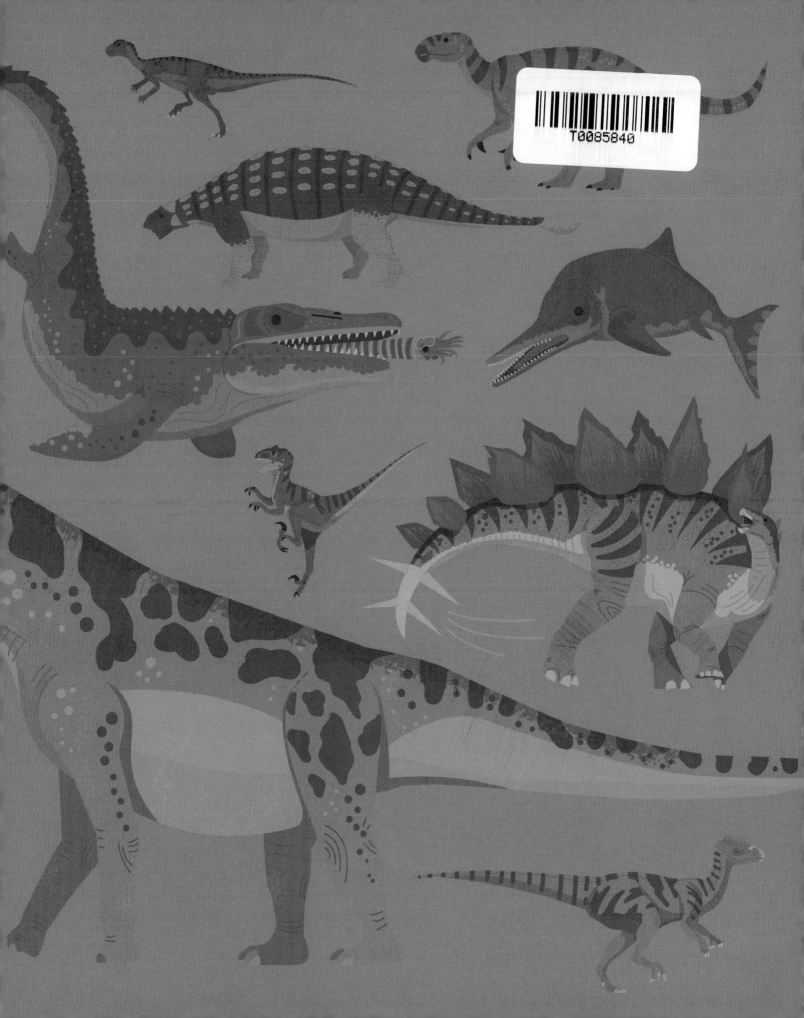

DINOSAURS!

DINOSAURS!

DINOSAURS!

DINOSAURS!
DINOSAURS!
DINOSAURS!

Happy Fox
BOOKS.

written by
SUSAN MARTINEAU

illustrated by
VICKY BARKER

For Alice and Will, my very own fact finders! - S.M

For Erick, my dinosaur super fan. - V.B

© 2024 Happy Fox Books, an imprint of Fox Chapel Publishing Company, Inc., 903 Square Street, Mount Joy, PA 17552.

Hardcover ISBN 978-1-64124-365-0
Paperback ISBN 978-1-64124-366-7

Library of Congress Control Number: 2023947127

To learn more about the other great books from Fox Chapel Publishing, or to find a retailer near you, call toll-free 800-457-9112 or visit us at www.FoxChapelPublishing.com.

We are always looking for talented authors. To submit an idea, please send a brief inquiry to acquisitions@foxchapelpublishing.com.

Fox Chapel Publishing makes every effort to use environmentally friendly paper for printing.

Printed in China

Contents

Welcome to dinosaur world

The dinosaurs lived MILLIONS and MILLIONS of years ago. It was long before any humans were alive, and our world looked very different then.

At first, the world was very hot and dry.

Then . . . after many millions of years . . .

. . . there was more and more rain. Tall trees and plants grew.

This time of the dinosaurs is called the **TRIASSIC PERIOD**.

Plateosaurus

Herrerasaurus

Stegosaurus

Coelophysis

Compsognathus

The word "dinosaur" means "terrible lizard."

Dinosaurs were amazing reptiles that lived on land.

Dinosaurs had claws on their hands and feet.

Later . . . after many more millions of years . . .

. . . the weather grew cooler. Now there were rainforests, and flowers bloomed.

This is called the **JURASSIC PERIOD.**

This was the **CRETACEOUS PERIOD.**

Tyrannosaurus Rex

Iguanodon

Allosaurus

Baryonyx

How big were the dinosaurs?

Many dinosaurs were as tall as a house.
They were the largest animals that ever
lived on land. But there were some
teeny dinosaurs, too!

Brachiosaurus
was taller than
three giraffes and
could eat from the
tallest trees.

Sinornithosaurus looked like
a dragon with feathers! It was
the size of a large turkey.

Triceratops was a very BIG-HEADED
dinosaur. It had three horns and
a fantastic frill.

Argentinosaurus was GIGANTIC! It was so big that it could only walk very slowly and could not run away!

Patagotitan was colossal! It had to eat nearly all the time to keep itself going.

I'm one of the biggest **titanosaurs** of all!

Diplodocus had a VERY long neck and a VERY long tail.

Hypsilophodon dashed on its long, slim legs, looking out for danger.

Compsognathus was one of the smallest dinosaurs and not much bigger than a chicken.

What did dinosaurs eat?

When you are as tall as a house, you need to eat a lot! Some dinosaurs ate each other, but others preferred to eat plants.

I am called an **herbivore** because I eat plants.

Diplodocus had teeth as long as pencils. They were really good for raking leaves off branches.

Herbivores had different-shaped teeth depending on what type of plants they ate.

Shantungosaurus had 1,500 teeth. Humans only have 32!

Anatotitan had wide, flat teeth for grinding up tough plants. Its mouth looked like a duck's bill.

Triceratops had hundreds of teeth like a wall with sharp ridges. These were perfect for chopping down plants.

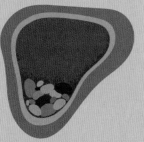

Some plant-eating dinosaurs also swallowed small stones, called **gastroliths**. The stones worked like teeth inside their stomachs. They helped mash up tough plants.

We eat meat.
We are **carnivores!**

Carnotaurus

Meat-eating
dinosaurs had
sharp, pointed
teeth. Ow!

Some **carnivores**,
like **Deinonychus**,
may have hunted
in packs.

Herrerasaurus

These fierce hunters
did not chew their food.
They just gobbled it up
in chunks!

Coelophysis

11

Watch out!

The scariest dinosaurs of all were called **theropods**.
These dinosaurs ran around on two legs and were very fierce hunters!

Velociraptor was REALLY speedy!

My name means "fast thief."

Baryonyx used its huge claws to hook fish out of rivers.

Allosaurus even ate each other!

Spinosaurus
could probably swim,
so it would have
munched on fish, too.

Deinonychus
had a long,
curved claw on
each foot, just
like a knife.

Giganotosaurus
might have been
even taller than
Tyrannosaurus Rex!

Look out for
Tyrannosaurus Rex
on the next page!

King of the dinosaurs

Tyrannosaurus Rex was the most frightening dinosaur on the planet. It had quite a big brain compared to other dinosaurs, so it was especially clever at hunting.

40 feet (12 m) long.

Claws on the end of its three gigantic toes.

T. Rex was not a picky eater. It also ate things that were already dead!

Very thick, strong neck.

Amazing sense of smell to sniff out lunch!

Teeth as long as a carving knife.

Small but strong arms.

Huge jaws with 60 curved, pointed teeth. These were serrated like a saw.

Two fingers with sharp claws.

Could easily crunch through bones!

Teeth could be up to 8 inches (20 cm) long.

Ready for a fight!

Some of the peaceful, plant-eating dinosaurs looked very fierce. This was because they needed to fight off the hungry **carnivores**.

Whack!

Ankylosaurus moved slowly and had a tail shaped like a club to whack attackers. It also had hard, bony lumps and spikes to protect itself.

Iguanodon had a secret weapon. Its thumbs had claws shaped like daggers.

Triceratops had three sharp horns and a huge frill around its neck to scare off **carnivores**. It could also gallop faster than a speeding rhinoceros.

Stegosaurus had long, sharp spikes on its tail and huge, bony plates on its back.

Centrosaurus and **Pachyrhinosaurus** had fantastic horns and frills.

Whoosh!

Pachycephalosaurus had a massive, bony head which would have been good for headbutting!

Einiosaurus had an incredible long, curved horn on its nose and spiky horns sticking out of its neck frill.

17

Dinosaur babies

Dinosaurs laid eggs, just like reptiles do today.
The mother dinosaurs laid them in nests on the ground.

Maiasaura
was a really
good mother.

My name means
"good mother
lizard."

The mother
Maiasaura stayed
on her nest to look
after her babies.

18

Maiasaura made nests close together. It was safer to be in a crowd!

Dinosaur eggs were different shapes and sizes . . .

. . . some were long and thin . . .

. . . and others were nearly round . . .

. . . some were as big as a human hand, and others as large as a football!

Many dinosaurs were too heavy to sit on their eggs. They probably piled plants and earth on top of them. This kept the eggs and hatchlings warm.

It is very rare to find a **fossil** of an egg with the baby dino inside!

Tyrannosaurus Rex babies were only about the size of a chicken when they hatched. They soon grew, though!

19

Growing up in dinosaur world

As soon as baby dinosaurs hatched, they started growing and growing and GROWING. They needed LOTS of food.

Some babies, like **Maiasaura**, stayed warm and cozy in their nest. Their mother brought them leaves and plants to eat.

We're hungry!

1. Baby **Maiasaura** were only 12 inches (30 cm) long when they hatched.

2. After six weeks, the babies were twice this size.

Huge, long-necked dinosaurs, like **Plateosaurus**, lived in groups. The babies probably walked in the middle of the herd. They were guarded by their enormous parents.

Other baby dinosaurs, like **Orodromeus**, had to look after themselves.

Mom? Dad? Where are you?

3. When they were one year old, they were 10 feet (3 m) long. This is 10 times bigger than when they hatched out of their eggs.

4. When they were grown up, **Maiasaura** were 30 feet (9 m) long! That's almost as long as a bus.

Under the sea

While the dinosaurs roamed on land, other strange and amazing creatures swam in the oceans and seas. They were not dinosaurs, even though some looked very much like them.

There were huge, underwater beasts called **plesiosaurs** and **ichthyosaurs**.

Plesiosaurs, like **Elasmosaurus**, had a very long neck like **Diplodocus** and the other long-necked **sauropods** on land. They also had . . .

. . . big flippers for pushing through the water while hunting for fish.

Ichthyosaurs, like **Stenopterygius**, were the same shape as a dolphin, but . . .

. . . they swam like a fish by sweeping their tails from side to side.

These ocean beasts were scary enough, but there were many more to watch out for if you were a little fish just minding your own business.

Sea crocodiles in dinosaur times had teeth like needles, ready to SNAP fish up.

Teleosaurus

Help!

Mosasaurs were like giant underwater lizards. They grew as large as whales!

Archelon was a gigantic turtle that was bigger than a rowboat.

Kronosaurus had a skull twice the size of **Tyrannosaurus Rex's**.

These sea beasts could not breathe under water. They had to come up to the surface to breathe air.

23

Flying through the air

Imagine seeing giant creatures gliding above your head!
There were many flying reptiles in dinosaur times, but they
were not dinosaurs. They are called **pterosaurs**.

Pterosaurs were **carnivores**,
and they liked to eat fish,
insects, and small reptiles.

Quetzalcoatlus was one of
the largest flying creatures
that has ever lived on Earth.
Its wings stretched as wide
as a small plane's, with a
wingspan of 39 feet (12 m)!

Pterodactylus was
a really speedy flyer.
It probably snacked on
insects as it swooped
through the air.

Pteranodon had a head
that was as long as the
height of a tall human.
Its wingspan was
23 feet (7 m)!

Dimorphodon had a head that looked a bit like a puffin's. Its beak may have been brightly colored, too.

Dsungaripterus liked eating shellfish and used its beak to hook them off rocks.

Rhamphorhynchus flew across the surface of the sea. It used its pointed, spiky teeth to scoop up fish.

Slurp!

Pterodaustro had a bristly bottom jaw! This was like a brush for filtering small creatures out of water.

Turned to stone

No one has ever seen a living dinosaur because they died so many millions of years before humans lived on Earth. We only know about them because of **fossils**.

Fossils are the stony remains of animals and plants that died a very long time ago. They are like clues showing us what the dinosaurs were like and what they did.

This is how dinosaur **fossils** were formed.

1.
A dinosaur died. Perhaps it was sick and fell into a lake. Layers of sand and mud washed over it.

2.
The dinosaur was completely buried. The soft parts of the body rotted away. All that was left were the hard bones.

Scientists have also found **fossils** of dinosaur poo so they can find out what the dinosaurs ate!

These poo **fossils** have a special name. They are called **coprolites**.

This took MILLIONS of years.

Dinosaur **fossils** are found all over the world in certain types of rock . . .

. . . like sandstone, clay, and limestone . . .

. . . often in deserts where the wind wears the rock away and uncovers the **fossils**.

3. More and more layers of sand and mud built up. They turned into rock, and the dinosaur bones turned into stone, too.

How exciting to spot one!

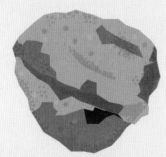

Bone left over from the dinosaur's meal!

27

Digging up dinosaurs

Dinosaur **fossils** are usually buried deep in rocks. They need to be carefully dug out. This can take years if scientists are lucky enough to find a whole dinosaur.

The scientists who dig up **fossils** are called **paleontologists**. They are like dinosaur detectives!

It is hard work . . .

. . . outside . . .

. . . and sometimes in very wild places.

They take lots of photos and measure everything really carefully.

The **paleontologists** also make a map of the digging area to mark exactly where they find the **fossils**.

28

What do the fossils show us?

Bones, teeth, and eggs—these tell us what the dinosaurs looked like.

Footprints and tracks—these show us what the dinosaurs did.

Scientists can work out how much a dinosaur weighed by looking at the depth of just one footprint and . . .

. . . how fast some dinosaurs could run by measuring the distance between footprints in a track.

New kinds of dinosaurs are being dug up all the time. Perhaps you will become a dino hunter and find one?

Dinosaurs with feathers!

When we think of the dinosaurs, we imagine they were all huge, scaly beasts, but some of them had feathers like birds.

Scientists have found **fossils** that show the long-necked dinosaurs, like **Haestasaurus**, had scales . . .

I have scaly skin like a lizard.

. . . BUT . . .

. . . other **fossils** show that some of the meat-eating dinosaurs had feathers!

Caudipteryx had a wonderful fan of feathers at the end of its tail.

Sinosauropteryx had feathery, winglike arms, but it could not fly.

Yutyrannus huali is the largest dinosaur with feathers that scientists have found so far. It was far too heavy to take off into the air.

Velociraptor had long arm feathers. These were not strong enough to be proper wings. Maybe the dinosaur used them to keep eggs warm on its nest.

Coloring in the dinosaurs

It is very hard to tell what color the dinosaurs were from looking at **fossils**.

But there might be some clues about this in the feather **fossils**. Scientists are working hard to find out more!

Archaeopteryx could probably fly a little bit, but it mainly ran around on its two legs.

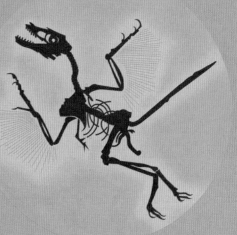

31

Dinosaurs on display

Dinosaur **fossils** are very precious and many are kept carefully in museums. Perhaps you have been lucky enough to see some yourself.

Back bones
(these are called **vertebrae**)

Skull

Clawed
hands

Ribs

Shin bone

TYRANNOSAURUS REX

Putting a dinosaur skeleton together is like doing a very old jigsaw puzzle with lots of pieces missing and no picture on the box!

Marks on **fossil** bones show the scientists how they fit together when the dinosaur was still alive.

Scientists use special machines to look inside the bones. This helps them understand more about the dinosaur.

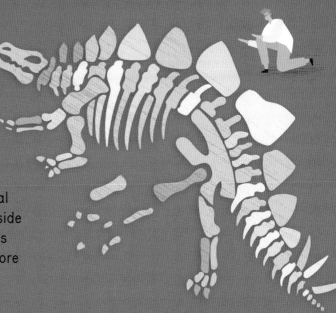

Thigh bone

Real **fossils** are often very fragile, so scientists make copies of them.

They can use these to make a model of how the dinosaur might have looked all those millions of years ago.

33

What happened to the dinosaurs?

All the very large dinosaurs suddenly disappeared around 66 million years ago. The flying **pterosaurs** and most of the sea reptiles vanished at the same time. What happened to them?

A monster rock from outer space whacked down on Planet Earth! BOOM!

Uh-oh! Watch out!

The mega-rock was a **meteorite**. Huge clouds of dust rose up into the sky.

The sunshine was blocked out, and plants and trees died.

The **herbivores** had nothing to eat. They died of hunger and cold.

Even the **carnivores** ran out of food. It was the end for them, too.

Scientists think that there were also lots of volcanoes erupting at the same time. It must have been very scary on Planet Earth!

Are there any dinosaurs left today?

Scientists know that some dinosaurs had feathers. Some of these dinosaurs did not die during the space-rock disaster.

Over millions and millions of years, these feathered dinosaurs gradually changed to become the birds that we see around us today. Birds are dinosaurs!

Special dinosaur words

Carnivore is an animal that only eats meat.

Coprolites are fossils of poo!

Cretaceous Period was the last part of the time of the dinosaurs.

Fossils are the stony remains of animals and plants that died a very long time ago.

Gastroliths are stones that dinosaurs swallowed to help break down food in their stomachs.

Herbivore is an animal that only eats plants.

Ichthyosaurs were a group of sea reptiles alive during the time of the dinosaurs.

Jurassic Period was the second part of the time of the dinosaurs.

Meteorite is a rock from space that lands on Earth.

Mosasaurs were a group of lizard-like sea reptiles alive during the time of the dinosaurs.

Paleontologist is a scientist who looks for fossils and investigates how dinosaurs lived.

Plesiosaurs were a group of long-necked sea creatures alive during the time of the dinosaurs.

Pterosaurs were a group of flying reptiles alive during the time of the dinosaurs.

Sauropod is the name given to all the long-necked plant-eating dinosaurs.

Theropod is the name given to the two-legged meat-eating dinosaurs.

Titanosaurs were the largest dinosaurs of all.

Triassic Period was the first part of the time of the dinosaurs.

Vertebrae are the bones that make up the spine of an animal.